CW00336278

Sewing at the

MANOR

Delightful Doves	2
Betty's Bed Runner	4
Cameo Cushion	6
Lizzy-Beth	8
Manor Mini Quilt	10
The Old Hall Stitchery	12
Six Pennies Candle Mat	13
Hints & Tips	14
Templates & Work Basket	14
We Raise our Glasses to...	17

Concentration Level

 Nice and relaxing... let's day dream

 This is fun

 Mmmm, let's think

✓✓✓✓ Put the coffee on, white no sugar

Florrie's Day at the Manor

Wake gently

Bathe and dress

Leisurely breakfast

Sew and read

Stroll in the grounds

Candlelit supper

Early night, warm bed

Betty's Day at the Manor

Up with the cockerel

Light the fires

Prepare the breakfasts

Cook and clean

Sweep the yards

Cook and clean

Collapse

Delightful Doves

There is a fabulous Dove Cote at the Old Hall and we took inspiration from this for our flying doves. If we are honest there is a touch of the Hilda O's about them too, if perhaps a little more tasteful! Our doves make an interior statement in any home.

What you need

(for one dove)

Fabric: 20cms

Toy Filling

2 x Small Buttons

Hanging Ring

Freezer Paper

Embroidery Thread

Finished Size: 7" x 7½" approx.

How to make one Dove

Make a Freezer Paper template of the dove on page 14.

Fold the fabric RST and iron on the template, sew around and cut out. Make a small slit in the back of the dove and turn through. Stuff the dove well and sew the opening closed.

Hand sew the wing details using embroidery thread, **see photo** for guidance.

Sew the small buttons onto the doves to create the eyes. Sew a ring onto the back of the dove for hanging. Make three doves for maximum effect.

Betty found it helpful to decide how she wanted the dove to hang before sewing on the ring, nothing worse than a wonky dove.

Why not?
Betty made several of the doves in bright colours and hung them from different length ribbons on the nursery ceiling. Her little one loves them!

BETTY'S POEM

Clarissa Clara Clutterbrook
Is the daughter of the Mayor
I'm sorry to say she is very spoilt
And doesn't seem to care
But one fine day I'm sorry to say
She will wake up and she will find
She hasn't got a single friend
For being so unkind

Betty's Bed Runner

The bedrooms at the Old Hall on the first floor are surprisingly bright and airy, in comparison to the servants sleeping quarters on the top floor. We have designed a bright bed runner to compliment the main bedroom but with a view to creating a contemporary item for the modern bedroom.

What you need

Fabric 1 (Green): 60cms

Fabric 2 (Gold): 40cms

Fabric 3 (Cream & Green): 20cms

Border Fabric: 25cms

Fabric 4 (Green Pattern): 20cms

Backing Fabric: 70cms

Wadding: 70cms

Binding: 40cms

Finished Size: 64" x 28"

Cutting

Fabric 1: Cut 24 x 5"squares and 12 x 2½" squares

Fabric 2: Cut 24 x 5" squares

Fabric 3 & 4: Cut 48 x 2½" squares from each fabric

Border Fabric: Cut 4 x 2½" strips WOF

Binding Fabric: Cut 5 x 2½" strips WOF

How to make it

Betty's Bed Runner is made up of 12 blocks which are constructed in the same way, but she has changed the placement of the fabrics slightly. The finished size of each block is 10". This could be easily made into a table runner or you could make more blocks and make a quilt for a bed. The instructions below are to make one block.

Take a Fabric 1 & Fabric 2 five inch square and place them RST. Draw a diagonal line on one of the pieces and sew a quarter inch either side of the drawn line. Now cut on the drawn line and press, trim the block to 4½" x 4½" and repeat to make 2 units.

Take a Fabric 3 & 4 square and sew them together, repeat to make a total of 4.

See photo and sew the units together, make a total of 6 units with the cream square next to the centre square (Fabric 1) and 6 units with the green square next to the centre square (Fabric 1) , refer to the photo for the placement of the fabrics.

Sew the completed blocks into two rows of 6 and then sew these rows together.

Sew border strips to the long sides and press. Now sew the remaining border strips to the top and bottom and press.

Layer Betty's Bed Runner with Wadding and the Backing Fabric and quilt your own design.

Once quilted bind the quilt using your own method or see the Work Basket.

Going to Pieces!?

Florrie and Betty would like to announce that worries about their sanity have been blown out of all proportion. The pieces they were referring to are shown below. These pieces make the preparation of the bed runner much easier.

Posh Jelly for Grown ups!

9 fl oz or 250ml of Tonic Water
3 ½ fl oz or 100ml of Gin
2 Gelatine leaves

Soften the gelatine leaves in a small dish of cold water.

Gently heat the tonic in a pan, add the drained leaves to the pan and stir until dissolved.

Add the gin. Add more gin or tonic depending on the flavour, Betty says you can't have enough gin, but that's Betty, make your own decision.

Pour this mixture into a container and set aside to cool. Pop in the fridge until set, usually about 4 hours.

Eat responsibly!

Cameo cushion

In the formal room at the Manor there are small Cameos on the walls. These were the period equivalent of our photographs today and are very charming. This Cameo cushion takes inspiration from these little works of Art.

What you need

Background Fabric: Fat Quarter	Fabric 3 (Silhouette): Fat 8th
Fabric 1 (scallop): 12" square	Backing Fabric: Fat Quarter
Fabric 2 (circle): 12" square	Heat 'n' Bond Feather Lite
Binding Fabric: 15cms	14" Cushion Pad

Finished Size: 14" approx.

How to make it

Cut the Background Fabric into a 16" square.

Trace the scallop, circle and silhouette onto the Heat 'n' Bond Feather Lite, cut out roughly and iron to the reverse of the relevant fabrics. Now cut them out on the drawn line.

Find the centre of the background fabric and position the scallop shape, fuse into place with the iron and sew using either a blanket stitch on the machine or it can be sewn by hand.

Now position the circle on top of the scallop, fuse and sew in place. Finally repeat this process with the silhouette.

Cut the cushion front to a 14½" square.

Cut the backing fabrics into two pieces 9½" x 14½". Hem one long edge of each piece.

Place these onto the reverse of the cushion front, wrong sides together, ensuring there is an over lap in the centre of the back, pin in place.

Prepare the binding by cutting 2 x 2½" strips. Sew these together to make one long strip. Bind using your usual method or see the Work Basket on page 14.

Insert your Cushion Pad.

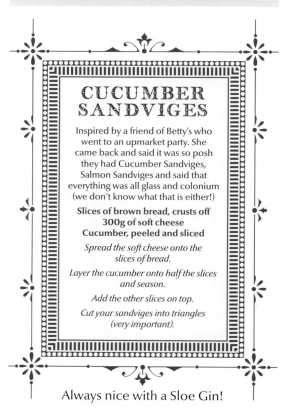

CUCUMBER SANDVIGES

Inspired by a friend of Betty's who went to an upmarket party. She came back and said it was so posh they had Cucumber Sandviges, Salmon Sandviges and said that everything was all glass and colonium (we don't know what that is either!)

Slices of brown bread, crusts off
300g of soft cheese
Cucumber, peeled and sliced

Spread the soft cheese onto the slices of bread.

Layer the cucumber onto half the slices and season.

Add the other slices on top.

Cut your sandviges into triangles (very important).

Always nice with a Sloe Gin!

Lizzy-Beth

Topsy Turvy dolls were popular in the period and great fun. Inspired by a small painting in the Hall of two small girls playing. We have made a Topsy Turvey Doll with the Lady of the Manor (Lizzie) on one half and a servant (Beth) on the other half.

What you need

Fabric A (Dark Purple): 70cms

Calico: 20cms

Toy filling

Fabric B (Light Purple): 70cms

Freezer Paper

Acylic Paint

Finished Size: 19″ x 16″ approx.

How to make it

Cut the Calico into 2 x 6″ x 16″ pieces and cut a 5″ x 16″ piece from Fabric A & B.

See photo (item 1) and sew the 4 pieces together and press. Fold the fabric in half lengthwise, matching the seams. (Florrie says make sure the same fabrics lie on top of each other).

Make Freezer Paper templates of the body and four arms on page 16. Place the templates on the fabric, **see photo** (item 2). Sew around the body and arms leaving openings where indicated on the template. Cut out using pinking shears and turn each piece to the right side. Stuff the heads and arms firmly but the bodies to cuddle-ability. Sew the openings on the body closed. Position the arms onto the body and sew in place.

To make the skirt cut a 15½″ x 28″ piece from Fabric A & B and a 5″ x 9½″ from Fabric A, this is the waistband.

Fold in the short edges of the waistband to the wrong side and press. Fold both long edges to centre, WST, and the fold in half again, and press. Place a pin a half inch in from each short side.

Place the larger Fabrics A & B RST and sew down 3 sides, leaving one long edge open. Turn through and press.

Keeping the raw edges together sew a gathering stitch along this edge. Gather to fit

the waistband within the pin markings. Place skirt piece into the waistband and sew in place, **see photo** (item 3).

Fold the skirt in half lengthwise, with the Fabric B on the outside and sew using a half inch seam allowance.

Fit the skirt to the doll with the seam of the skirt centred at the back. Hand stitch in place.

Using the pattern on page 16 draw in the hair and paint using acrylic paint and allow to dry.

ITEMS FOUND IN BETTY'S LAUNDRY

Mysterious items have turned up in Betty's Laundry as detected by Sgt Biff. She had been offering a laundry service for the local law inforcement. Members of the public can rest at ease as the needle has now been removed safely from Sgt Biff's behind. The items in question are below.

ITEM 1

ITEM 2

ITEM 3

RANTER TERRIE

Ranter the farm terr was seen lying in the haystack chewing o a bone whilst the ra played beside him. The Master couldn' understand how a b designed for ratting could do this, until h found out Miss Flor had been using him as a lap dog. She jus doesn't understand boundaries

Schizophreni Doll With Sp Personality

Lizzie- Beth, split personality?
Miss Lizzie 'that lazy maid Beth is an inso little madam, she thin she runs the house ar sometimes forgets he She has to remember her place'
Beth 'what she forge is that we are so alike anyone would think could be the same per

Wash Day Bl

Wash day blues
Miss Betty was over to exclaim that her n dove cote was the tal of the village. Her do were so beautiful. He maid took a different view, she had spent h washing the laundry hanging it out to dry, dove's by product wa quite so appealing.

Florrie's Bit on the Side

Real life extracts from Florrie's Memories....

Me mam remembers going up to a country house in Lancashire when she was a bairn. Once a year they could go up there for lemonade and cake, her Aunt worked in the kitchen there as an under cook. She didn't like to too much because she had to wear her Sunday best and she used to wipe her boots on the table cloth!

We had a dove house, me dad made it. Me mam always loved to see the doves, I think she would have loved those white doves to live in it but we had a couple of skemies who came every year and had at least four broods, they were prolific breeders, them pigeons! I used to love watching the chicks leave for the first time, so cautious and never straying too far.

CHRIST PRESEN

One Christmas doll with a chin She had a sligh open mouth and my mind was q beautiful. Me c got a doll too, s lived next door time and was sp rotten. She dec she didn't like h doll and wanted and me mam said I had swop. I was so I pushed a stick her open mouth wedged there ju of reach.
Well we swopp I got the cloth d she had, but bec I'd ruined the o doll she change mind.
I spent the rest c childhood tryin get the stick out her mouth.

The Manor Mini Quilt

In front of the Manor House is a pretty formal garden. We took this as the inspiration for our lovely little doll quilt. It is the perfect addition to any dollies bed but would look equally good as a cushion or why not make several of them to make a larger quilt.

What you need

Fabric for Centres: (Cream) Fat 8th

Fabric 1: (Red) 20cms

Fabric 2: (Blue) 15cms

Fabric 3: (Green) 15cms

Border 1 & Binding: 20cms

Border 2: 10cms

Backing: 60cms

Wadding: 60cms

Finished Size: 20″ approx.

How to make it

We will give you the instructions to make a flying geese unit, you will then make the number of units using the correct colour combinations. The large rectangle is called the goose and the small squares create the sky. Your cutting recipe is on the opposite page.

Draw a diagonal line on the reverse of two 2½″ squares. Place one on a 4½″ x 2½″ unit, RST and sew on the drawn line. Cut away the excess fabric to make a quarter of an inch seam on the square and press. Repeat with the other square on the opposite side. **See photo** for the stages of sewing and cutting.

Now make 8 Blue geese units and 8 Green geese units with red skies (Fabric 1).

Make 4 Red geese units each with a half blue and half green sky, **see photo**.

Refer to the photo and lay out all of your flying geese units and squares to match.

The quilt is made up of 5 rows, **see photo**.

Sew each row together taking care to match your points Florrie often uses pins and has found that if she presses her seams open she gets a better finish. Now sew all the rows together to create the quilt top. At this stage it should measure 16½″.

Sew the short pieces of the Border 1 fabrics to opposite sides, press open and then sew the remaining two on. Repeat this for the Border 2 fabrics.

Layer the quilt with the wadding and backing and quilt as desired. Trim to size and bind. using your favourite method. See Work Basket.

Cutting

Centres Fabric: Cut 5 X 4½″ Squares

Fabric 1: Cut 4 X 4½″ X 2½″; 32 X 2½″ X 2½″

Fabric 2: Cut 8 X 4½″ X 2½″; 6 X 2½″ X 2½″

Fabric 3: Cut 8 X 4½″ X 2½″; 6 X 2½″ X 2½″

Border 1: Cut 2 X 1″ X 16½″; 2 X 1″ X 17″

Border 2: Cut 2 X 2″ X 17″; 2 X 2″ X 20″

Binding: Cut 2 X 2½″ Strips Wof

Backing: Cut A 23″ Square

Wadding: Cut A 23″ Square

The Old Hall Stitchery

Little girls would practice their sewing and embroidery skills by making beautiful samplers. Our simple design is a nod to this pastime and shows the front of the Old Hall. By designing it as a stitchery, it is quick and easy to achieve.

What you need

Fabric: Fat Quarter

Weaveline: Fat Quarter

Embroidery Thread

Frame 11" x 8" (Optional)

Finished Size: 11" x 8" approx.

How to make it

Iron the Weaveline to the reverse of the fabric. Trace the stitchery on page 15 and stitch using 2 strands of embroidery thread. Now trim to 12" x 9" to fit your frame.

Florrie and Betty have added the stitches you need to complete this stitchery in the below newspaper clipping, they might come in very handy. Watch those fingers!

oung Mel

oung Mel, the maid's son was eard complaining about the job of one picking from the ploughed elds. Miss Florrie was astonished o later see him throwing the same tones at the jackdaws on the ield to scare them away when the arley had been sown. Self defeating or what!

To stitch or not to stitch?
The age old question has never fully been addressed.
The answer lies with the individual and in this post modern, de-constructing age we live in, the problem is taken to the next level.
   But hey life is too short, get your needle and threads out and give it a go, you never know you might enjoy it!

FRENCH KNOT DIAGRAM

BACK STITCH DIAGRAM

RUNNING STITCH DIAGRAM

may your bobbin

always be full

Six Pennies Candle Mat

One of the activities the staff carry out at the Old Hall is the making of tallow candles. Candles are hugely popular again in the modern home although we are very lucky to have the choice! We have made a lovely felt candle mat incorporating our signature Six Pennies.

What you need

Black Felt: Fat Quarter

Green Felt: 10cms

Embroidery Thread

Six Small Buttons

Freezer Paper

Finished Size: 9″ Diameter.

How to make it

Make Freezer Paper templates of 2 large and 6 small circles on page 14 and cut out of the felts, **see photo**. Place the small circles onto one of the large ones and blanket stitch in place.

Add the second large circle to the reverse and stitch the outer edge to hold them together.

Add six small buttons, **see photo**.

Florrie likes to use a blanket stitch when she sews with felt. She sometimes adds decorative stitching as well.

Templates & Work Basket

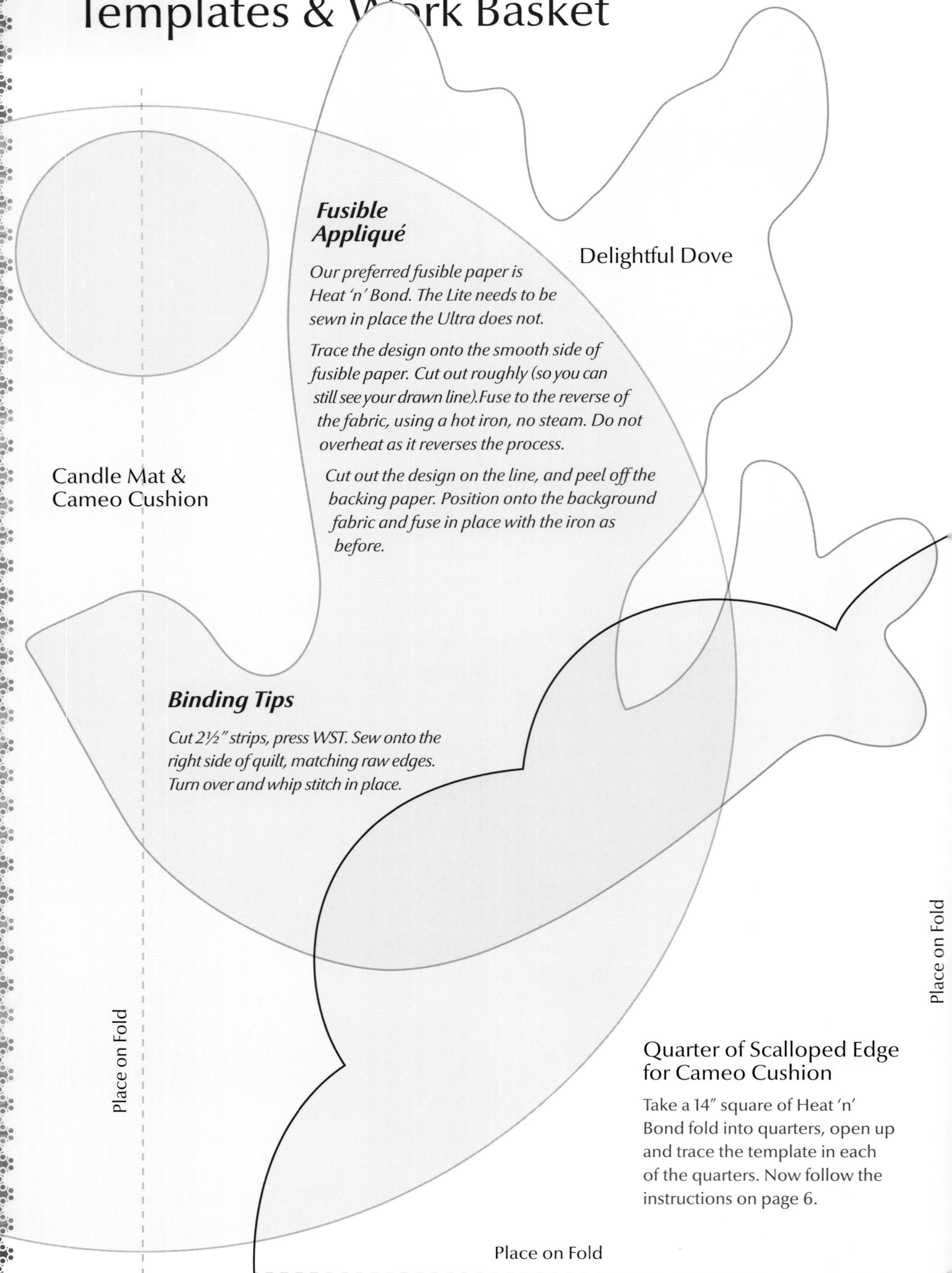

Fusible Appliqué

Our preferred fusible paper is Heat 'n' Bond. The Lite needs to be sewn in place the Ultra does not.

Trace the design onto the smooth side of fusible paper. Cut out roughly (so you can still see your drawn line). Fuse to the reverse of the fabric, using a hot iron, no steam. Do not overheat as it reverses the process.

Cut out the design on the line, and peel off the backing paper. Position onto the background fabric and fuse in place with the iron as before.

Delightful Dove

Candle Mat & Cameo Cushion

Binding Tips

Cut 2½" strips, press WST. Sew onto the right side of quilt, matching raw edges. Turn over and whip stitch in place.

Place on Fold

Place on Fold

Quarter of Scalloped Edge for Cameo Cushion

Take a 14" square of Heat 'n' Bond fold into quarters, open up and trace the template in each of the quarters. Now follow the instructions on page 6.

Place on Fold

may your bobbin

always be full

Templates & Work Basket

Cameo Cushion

Lizzy-Beth

Leave Open

Lizzy-Beth
Leg

Is Size an Issue?

Apparently so, there is always confusion over imperial and metric measurements so here is a helpful guide.

10cm = 4"

What does it mean?

RST means Right Sides Together
WST means Wrong Sides Together
WOF means Width of Fabric

Leave Open

Place on Fold